Timeless Avatar Press

Florida*London*Vancouver

Also, by Sara Degraff

How to Dance with Life (essays)

Nighttime (Poetry)

Songs of Hope (Anthology of Poetry)

The Hands of our Community (Anthology of Essays)

Table of Contents

Copyright Page vii
Dedication viii
Gratitude ix
Preface x
Reviews xi
    I xi
    II xii
    III xiii
Today 1
Here I am 2
I am tired of dancing 3
Running Late 4
Where does time go? 5
I was born to leave my mark 6
I am one step closer 7
Living without regrets 8
This is not my home 9
Will the dream disappear if I wake up? 10
With not much…youth…to spare 11
Heartbreak in Paris 12

Time is as long as eternity 13
Please do not cry! 14
I thought in your embrace 15
Would you give me a chance? 16
Win me over 17
Do not walk away! 18
Away from you 19
Was it necessary? 20
A glimpse… a taste… so sweet 21
Why do I still love you? 22
My heart calls your name 23
Can we take a walk 24
You pulled me close 25
Throw me a lifeline 26
Baby 27
Betrayal and Misery… 28
Approachable… 29
He was my first 30
In Matters of Love 31
His eyes locked with mine 32
When I survive this round 33
Nothing worth waking up for 34
Lonely hearts 35
Longing for the love of a child 36

I am an untold story 37
I live in a hidden world 38
I am a quiet storm 39
The scent of Happiness 40
When I unclothe myself 41
The Wind of Hope 42
My Heart goes out to Haiti 43
Coming from a far 45
I do not want to wake up flawed 46
The angry Gods 47
Face to Face 48
I remember a little spring 50
Walking the same grounds as my ancestors 51
It was only yesterday 52
What Should I Say? 53
Fate plays tricks 54
At this stage of the race 55
Some say 56
This is the "Thanks" I get 57
Defying all logic 58
There was a dark cloud 59
While you were sleeping 60
We were sisters 61
I hope to see you in my dreams 62

Everybody leaves anyway 64
God will make a way 65
I will praise you forever… 66
It all started with many empty nights 67
Thank you, Lord, ... 68
I call upon the grace of God to cover me 69
I call upon my energy 70
I will not let go! 71
Longtemps je t'ai attendu 72
D'un clignement d'oeil rapide 73
Can you wash away the scent of the other woman? 74
Epouse effaçée 75

Copyright Page

Heartfelt copyrighted in June 2025 by Timeless Avatar Press.
ISBN # 978-0-978-1567-6-3

All rights reserved. It is prohibited to reproduce or transmit any part of this book in any format without permission from the author.

Dedication

My "Heartfelt" book is dedicated to Joubite Dessalines: My greatest source of inspiration and motivation. His unwavering support and belief in me made all this possible.

Gratitude

I thank God for guiding me through my journey

And the invisible forces that protect me

I thank my parents for welcoming me into this world
and for guiding my steps into the diversified classrooms of life

I thank my corporeal vessel that I could never have done without.

I thank my siblings, relatives and friends for motivating me.

I am grateful for the lessons I've learnt in hard and good times, that taught me about the duality of life.

I thank the kind strangers who brightened my journey with kind words, and smiles

I thank you for welcoming Heartfelt into your life.

Preface

From the depth of her soul, Sara expresses peace in a turbulent world, hope in the sparkling and rhythmic songs of her beloved Africa where she once lived, in the heart where the unspoken desires reside, and in God whom she awaits in the stillness of the night. Love in Heartfelt is like a kaleidoscope that reveals various colorful images of a faith in God that has no bound. It is a light that illumines our relationships with one another.

Heartfelt is a sensitive, earnest expression of Sara's love for life, the pleasure felt in the tender embrace of a lover in the affection that she has for her family, in the desires of her heart, and in the fleeting thoughts of her mind.

Dr Leslie G. Desmangles

Reviews

I

Heartfelt is a book of poems written with unfiltered honesty and emotions. The author navigates through various emotions and her life experiences as her blueprints. Each poem depicts her love for life, her faith in God and respect for her ancestors.

Despite her many heartbreaks and betrayals, her fighting spirit never wavers, she thrives and longs for more.

Sara Dessalines

II

Heartfelt by Sara DeGraff is quiet, yet powerful exploration of human connection and the small moments that define us. Poems from the heart for moral support and comfort of the soul stand for the good of all.

Emotions are raw. Progress is slow. But that's the point. DeGraff shows how sincerity isn't about grand gestures or dramatic revelations. It's in the small, uncomfortable truths we often avoid. DeGraff's writing is simple but precise. She captures the weight of unspoken words and the way people can heal without even realizing it.

What makes this book stand out is its honesty. It doesn't promise easy answers or perfect endings. Instead, it shows how life moves forward, one small step at a time. If you're looking for a story that feels like a quiet conversation with a friend, this is it.

It's not about grand gestures. It's about the moments in between the ones that stay with you long after you've turned the last page.

Reverend Nathanael Louis Barnabé Saint-Pierre

III

Heartfelt whispers soft and true
A tender dance in shades of blue
With every line, her words take flight
Like stars that pierce the darkest night.
A book of love, joy, and pain,
Like gentle drops of summer rain.
Each page a sigh, each rhyme a kiss,
A fleeting touch of heartfelt bliss.
The ink runs deep, the feelings soar,
A heart laid bare forevermore.
Like whispered songs on evening air,
Her poems show how much she cares.
So, open up and take a part
This treasure called Heartfelt, a work of art

Steeves Gino Belance

IV

Heartfelt by Sara DeGraff is a symphony of nuanced themes. A stirring collection of poems, the book delves into the values of time, love, loyalty, family, youthful alacrity and Pan-African emancipation. Through each verse, the poet entwines her soul with the universe to create rhythms that speak to the realities of contemporary world. HEARTFELT, we feel you.

Odima Osure

Today

I give myself to myself

Today I cease to be

The isolated tree in the wilderness

Both of us embark on the boat of life

Where our hearts linked forever

Contemplate the beauty of the spectacle

Here I am

In my full glory
Resplendent
All Broken
Pieces fallen into places
Stepping into the shoes
Of my destiny
In my full glory
A woman of value
No more hiding
Running
Forward
No more lazing
in my backyard
Too afraid to be seen
Steering clear of prying eyes
And all the…
"Where have you been?
No more lies…
No more hiding my face
Such an amazing grace!!!
Finally, all scattered pieces
Of me have come into one
I am now fine on my own

I am tired of dancing

Dancing in the dark
Losing track
Wasting valuable time
I am tired of dancing
Dancing in the dark
Losing spark
Waiting for my big break
Gasping…

Running Late

Fate is waiting at the gate
At this rate
If I do not hurry
I will be sorry
That state of mind
I find myself in
My life...mostly nights
Long rainy days
Unnecessary delays
Unfulfilled dream
My soul crushed
Is it fate?
Should I learn to hate
For being broken
Forgotten or for time stolen
Should I bid farewell
Or strive to live well?
Era of live streaming
Distorted views...
Strangers following...
From afar, emotions...
Feelings laid bare...
Sacrificed on
The altar of fake news
With nowhere to hide
What should one do?
That sinking feeling!!!
The burden of time!!!

Where does time go?

The time when you were the idol
And the light of your people
The time when everyone bowed
At the mere mention of your name
Already, there are other hymns, other rhythms
Where does time go?
The time when you shed your blood
Fighting for those cursed people
Already, you are tossed aside!
Today, here you are
In a highland Lying incognito
Away from the sun

I was born to leave my mark

However, life is not a walk
Through the park
One easily can fall on the wrong side of the tracks
I was born to leave my mark
First, I had to learn to swim with sharks
Am I in the right ballpark?
Would I have my life back?
Note to myself:
Act more, react less, harness my power
Be better!
Do not wither!
I was born to leave my mark!
Give me my life back!

I am one step closer

No turning back
Struggling through
Either win or lose
If anything happens
Do not worry
Whatever is broken
Can be mended
Cried a river
In search of my happily ever after
It had to rain
To wash out the pain
From the darkest nights
Come the brightest stars
I am one step closer
When the party is over
The curtain drawn
The audience has left
There can be no regrets

Living without regrets

Having a few pets
Humming out of joy
Finally living…
Not merely existing
Living without regrets
Having such perfect
And fulfilling life
Letting go of all strife
Living without regrets
Enjoy to the fullest
Anything
Happening
Exciting
That ever caught my eyes
A shooting star…
Blue sky stretched forever
A life fully experienced
Living without regrets…

This is not my home

My home is a castle built
On top of a mountain overlooking below
Giving access to only a chosen few
This is not my garden
In my garden
Sunflowers and Moonflowers
Grow side by side
This is not my face
Who is this caricature frowning at me
In the mirror?
This is not my music
I've never played those notes before
I've never danced to that tune before
This is not my life!!!
Everything looks so unfamiliar
This is not my journey
Somewhere along the way
I might have gotten Lost

Will the dream disappear if I wake up?

Will my journey be lighter?
If I close the doors of the past?
Being pulled into the light
Forbidden to look back
To avoid falling into a dark abyss
Fighting a war without weapons
Being tossed aside
Feeling hurt inside
How do I climb the mountain of hope?
Will someone throw me a rope
So, I can reach the top?
Great things await me there!
All my tears have been used up!
Will the dream disappear if I wake up?
Will my future change
With my eyes wide open?

With not much...youth...to spare

Much happiness to share
Body and soul laid bare...
My most precious treasure
On call merely for your pleasure
Listening to my heart's promptings
Romance sparkling
Then, you made me cry...
I tried to get by...
Naked in the face of the unknown
Spirit shattered into fragments...
The Thorns of Love!!!

Heartbreak in Paris

Baby what gave you the right
To steal my heart
And tear it apart?
You could have "hold me" tight
To help me through the night.
Instead, you kept me out of sight
At every turn, you stomped on my heart
You could have given me a head start?
After all I was all alone
Not made of stone
The deck already stacked against me
The coldness of time!!!

Time is as long as eternity

And
Eternity
Is
On my side
For
Eternity
Is
Nothing
But
That boundless space
Where the now… the yesterdays
And
Tomorrow
Are just one

Please do not cry!

Hold back the tears
It is not over
As long as your heart beats
There is hope
So, try to cope
Lift your head
And charge ahead
As long as your heart beats
There is a way
A path forward
Do not cry
The limit is the sky
It may be dark now
The sun will soon come out

I thought in your embrace

I would find solace
I thought that your presence
Would exult peace
Rather It brought Sadness...
Restlessness...
Unhappiness...
It breaks my heart
To say Goodbye!
May the force
Be with you!

Would you give me a chance?

Would you give me a chance?
If I made a mistake?
Would you catch me
Or let me fall
If I stumbled?
Would you color my days?
Brighten my nights?
When life gets too hectic
Would you leave me behind?
Would you be there?

Win me over

No longer
Under the cover
Of searching for happiness
Will I let you be heartless!
Win me over
Once again
Be my lover
Baby be mine!
Win me over
Be gentler... try softer!
Win me over...
Together
Let's go there!

Do not walk away!

If you do
You will take away
My everything...
Despite all your unkept
Promises and heartbreaks
Knowing that you were
Somewhere happy
Even with someone else
Made my heart skip a beat
Why don't you just stay?
Find a way
To be
In each other's arms again?
Do not just walk away!
From afar things
May seem chaotic
If given time
Our bush may blossom
Into beautiful sunflowers
Please baby stay…
Let's find a way!

Away from you

I feel lost and empty
Inside my heart
There is the frenziest tempest
I tremble and mumble
The melody of dizzy birds
Hoping for a presage
From a pilgrim dreamer

Was it necessary?

By any chance did you mistake me for an enemy?
With a smile on your face, you tore my world apart
I gave you my heart lightened by passion...
My most precious possession
You sacrificed it on the altar of stardom
Was it boredom?
Baby, at what cost?
I could have been lost
Was my pain your gain?
Anyone's gain?
Did it make you reach new heights?
Did it make anyone happy?
Did it make you happy?

A glimpse... a taste... so sweet...

Because it is forbidden fruit
Whichever way I want it?
Whenever I crave it?
From head to toe will it do?
Oh no!
Unless it is fully mine
It will be out of line
Rather fasting than tasting
Either sweet or bitter
I want my own not merely a loan
I choose longevity over frivolity
Whatever is forbidden
Must remain hidden...forgotten
Until ready for use
But I know that nothing
Or no one can outshine
The sun brightness
Nor prevent it from piercing
Through the clouds
Revealing what is in the dark

Why do I still love you?

Why do I still love you when should I hate you?
You make happy then you break my heart
Why do I still love you when you are so cruel?
You drive me crazy then you break it again
I am left in pain
One look into your eyes, I am at your mercy
Why do I still love you?
Please tell me...Tell me why?
Either you are all in or you are out?
My heart will go on...
No need to dress my wounds
If not around to help heal the scars
I will love again...
Your loss will be someone's gain

My heart calls your name

I feel so lame
Even ashamed
How could it
Betray me
After you stomped
On it?

Can we take a walk

Have a little talk?
Take a chance
Have the last dance?
If I start bumbling
My memories start failing me
Would you spice things up bring our passion back
Would you remind of our steamy love affair?
If my eyes start failing me
And it became all dark in my world
Would you become my light?
Illuminate my nights?
Would you be there?

You pulled me close

Just because you were
In a conquest mode
I created a bubble, but it popped
Being a lover like no other
You pulled me closer
How could I have known?
I had hardened up
Sworn up and down
No matter how mind-blowing the love
It wouldn't withstand my resolve
But all my reluctance crumbled
You never deserved me
You were nothing
But a frenzy passing though
It is well with my soul
I am nobody's foul
Mr. Wrong
Because I am Ms. Strong!

Throw me a lifeline

While I am being sidelined
My life put through the wringer
While letting go of all anger
Yes, still victim of destiny
Sense of humor
Rumor has it…
Nothing but rumor…
That I have nothing left in the pipeline
Nothing left in my tank
This is such a prank!!!
Throw me a lifeline
I am not doing fine
It hurst inside
When no one is on your side
My road paved with betrayal
Feeling as if life is slipping away
Vengeance is not the way
The true pathway to survival
Is to stand tall…
To find lasting peace
Never waver in the face of injustice!

Baby

Be my toy… give me joy for the night
Do not forget to turn off the light
Tonight… wanna be freaky
Be ready to make me sing
Wanna whine on something
You think that I am your ATM
Not trying to put any blame
Too bad I am not your flame
Feeling no shame
Give it to me without measure
My little vendor of pleasure
No more talk about feeling
Do your thing!!!
You are nothing
But a vendor of ride
No longer thinking
Being your bride
Tonight, I can't be shy
I want to buy something hot
Give me a whisky shot
Better move that waist
I don't want my money to go to waste
Tonight, it is about thrust
Not trust
Stormy skies
Too many lies…
Bluer skies coming…
Ahead smooth sailing…
Birds chirping!
Roosters crowing!
Calm breeze!
The breeze
of anticipation!

Betrayal and Misery...

Go hand in hand
Beg for forgiveness
And true blessings will befall
You will walk tall
With your head high
Stop the lie!

Approachable...

Non-exclusive...
Reckless heart!!!
Some things are sacred
Defile them
And disrupt the rhythm of the Universe

He was my first

Guided me through many firsts
First embrace
First kiss
First touch
A love waiting to burst out
He was my first
First betrayal
First heartbreak
My innocence trampled upon …
He was my first
First wrong choice
A past which cannot be erased
A reminder of what
Could have been: "A newborn first cry"
"Fond memories of a not so lonely existence"

He was my first
For each one of my hopes crushed
A needle in his dreamlike
Pitiful-make-believe life
Nothing but a mirage!
He was my first
Deep seated regrets…resentments
Still hard to bid farewell
A lover torn into pieces
A victim of his own karma!

In Matters of Love

Anything goes some say
I say no way
Love is not a game
This is the meeting of two hearts
In matters of love
Others believe this is all about winning
I beg to differ
When two hearts come together
If one hurts so does the other
They either win or lose as one

His eyes locked with mine

My eyes lost in his
The hope of a possibility
The eyes of my heart upon his gaze
A window to his soul
A true heart to heart connection
Mine longed for his
His reached out, miles across oceans
My eyes, from afar watching his sweet
Tongue savoring luscious lips
Giving into his most basic instincts
Tempted and defeated human frailty
His eyes wandered but never left me
He incessantly reached out to me
Through soft embrace his arms comforted many
His healing hands gave hope to the marginalized
He was a good man!

When I survive this round

I will create lasting bounds
The kinds that create lasting memories
When I survive this round
There will be plenty of nights out of town
Prayers of thankfulness
Out of that nothingness
All the restlessness
Feeling down still I bloom
When I survive this round
I will not be thrown
I will stand my ground
I will be unstoppable
And more than capable
To turn on my own light
A light so bright…so very bright
That will frighten my enemies
When I survive this round
My life will be a fully blown experience
Not merely a glance
At its scenery

Nothing worth waking up for

Nothing but a downpour
I asked: "Should I fall
Build a wall?"
A shimmer of hope
Will it help me cope?
In my hours of solitude
I confide in the many quiet
Waters of the Universe
In my hours of melancholy
I long for a time
When the sun and the stars will shine
A time
When my music mingling
With the singing
Of the birds
Will announce dawn

Lonely hearts

Searched for each other in the dark
And there was no child
No one to honor thy name
No one to carry our torch
No one to tell our tales
Our children are dying
No one to hail our ancestors
No one to lay us asleep
No one to carry our legacy
Our children are dying
Another starless night
Lonely hearts
Searched for each other In the dark
And there was no child

Longing for the love of a child

Longing for a needle in a haystack
The love of a child: An impossible dream
For barren woman I am called
So many unwanted children!!!
Longing for the warm embrace
Of a nurturing mother
The cruelty of Life!
Longing for a relationship
Not merely a friendship
A fulfilling...
Exhilarating...
Ice melting feeling
The quest for perpetual happiness!

I am an untold story

Let me tell you
How I scurry confidently through the rain
To overcome excruciating pain
Let me tell you how I found happiness
How I found joy to fill the emptiness
I just believed…I just surrendered…
I just found my own happiness
Inside myself to fill the loneliness
I am an untold story…
Let me tell you now…
How I scurry through the rain

I live in a hidden world

Never traveled by many
A world surrounded by trees of the unknown
I travel through bumpy roads and wild rivers
Roads only seen and rivers only
Crossed by a few throughout my pilgrimage
My suitcase amassed dust
Dirt got stuck to my shoes of Greatness
And made my steps heavy-laden
Throughout my journey
I traveled through roads
Only dreamt by many

I am a quiet storm

I am a warrior spirit
I am a pilgrim dreamer
longing for bluer skies
I am a leafless tree
Standing on
An unrhythmical world
I am a quiet storm

The scent of Happiness

Once again, I am wearing it
Once again, I am soaked in it
For a long time, happiness played
Hide and seek with me
I searched for it everywhere
Under the cover…
On the coffee table…
On the back seat of a car …
Hoping to fly
And reaching for the sky
The scent of Happiness can be quite elusive
Now that is within grasp, I will be ruthless
Remove all stumbling blocks
The scent of happiness is magic
It can be contagious…
Make lots of jealous
Guard it!

When I unclothe myself

When I unclothe myself of my corporeal vehicle
Who will accompany it to its final dwelling?
Who will shed a tear?
Those left behind will I be able
To ease their pain from beyond?
Will I be missed?
How will I be remembered?
Beyond the gate of eternity
Who will be there to welcome me?
When I cross that bridge?
Will I get to meet all those who left before me?
Those I did not get to bid farewell
In my next life who will be there with me?
Those I did not get to see in this lifetime
Will our path ever cross again?
My parents, siblings, friends, lovers
In my next incarnation, will they be there
As blessings or lessons?
Hopefully there is still time to live my best life
Leave no stone unturned...
Get answers to my deepest burning questions:
Who Am I? Why Am I here?
When comes my moment of truth
I want to be at peace and be able to say:
I came, I saw, I Learned...
And gave it a fighting chance

The Wind of Hope

The Wind of Hope Blowing my way
Bouncing through my heart
Beneath the Blazing Sun of Africa
The leaves dancing...
Rustling as if humming a sacred song
To welcome a prodigal daughter
The beat of tam-tam as if coming
From a parallel world
Setting my soul on fire
A shiver went down my spine
I was home
The Unbreakable Bound

My Heart goes out to Haiti

As her daughter I am one
Of those who betrayed her
One of those who deserted her
She has invested in me
When push came to shove, I ran away
There was a sense of imminent danger!
On the brink of disaster
All odds against her
It was a "sauve qui peut moment"
What would you have done?
Stay and fight?
Fight with whom?
The invisible hands
Hiding behind the curtains
Arming our children
Destroying our institutions?
What would you have done?
Offer sacrifices?
Perform rituals?
Pay the spiritual debt of our independence
For unkept promises to spirits invoked...?
This was too much responsibility
For an innocent teenager...
I still remember
How the almond tree

At Uncle Juan and Auntie Celina
Shed me from the afternoon hot sun
I still remember the taste of mango "fil"
Apricot... Corossol and Labapen...
Childhood Memories of my late younger brother:
Dancing in the rain... racing...competing...
Trying to out run each other... fly our kites...
Are still incredibly vivid.
I left... but not without amertume!
I grieved all those left behind
Some, I never got to see again
Especially Mom waving goodbye...
Inconsolable at the airport
With that flowery brown dress
That late July afternoon...
Unaware that was truly Goodbye!!!

Coming from a far

The beat of Tam-Tam
Thunder crashing
Unbridled spasm
Throughout my body
Who am I?
Who have I become?

I do not want to wake up flawed

I do not want to get up floored
I want to be whole again
Be alive again...
That soothing and rare feeling
Of long... long time ago
I want to feel it once more
I want to wake up flawless
Befriend happiness
Live without pain
And not be knocked down again!

The angry Gods

Have turned my body
Into a horse to gallop
Into forbidden alleys
The Goddess of Love
Has tied my hands
Opened my love garden
For malicious and mocking souls
To come and let their hair down
Some powerful forces
Are playing chess with my life

Face to Face

Face to face with the spirits of my ancestors
I kneel with reverence
You see...
In the eyes of the ancestors
I am the culprit who has neglected "The Lakou"
For long ago I became the chosen
As my maternal high priestess
Grandma was transitioning
She said: "When I am gone,
I want you to replace me"
At 11 years old, what did I know?
I only knew the sound of
The drum speaks to my soul...
Each beat makes my body gyrate
Transports me to ecstasy
As it moves to its vibration...
Twenty years later, my paternal uncle
A high priest himself took me as a pupil
And confirmed Grandma's choice
While satisfying my hunger
For traditional and cultural values
I learned that unique gifts
Are only given to the wise ones
That the greater the gifts

The greater the trials and tribulations
There are rites of passage...
And Rules are not to be violated
Suddenly two "Lakou" claimed me
Which way to go, I asked myself?
Fascinated and scared to lose my soul
As my catholic upbringing would have me believed
I had one foot in and one foot out
Never fully there... Never fully out...
I lift my eyes up begging for deliverance
Who will rescue me?
In the eyes of the ancestors
I am the one to carry the torch
Why aren't they guiding me?
My head is filled with hymns
From the God of my youth
With images of lengthy
Saint Joseph and Virgin Mary Processions
My head is bombarded with rhythms
From the drum hailing to the ancestors
The savory smells of Rêve d' Or, Pompeia
Florida Water ... Bien être...
The scents of burnt myrrh, Afetida offerings...
Rhums and Clair in mixed with dirt still haunt me
Face to Face with the spirits of my ancestors
I kneel with reverence
Lifting my eyes up asking
For deliverance and guidance...
Memories of the God of my youth
And the Gods of my ancestors are still intertwined
The battle for my soul!

I remember a little spring

From the birthplace of my mother
I remember the birds
Singing at dawn
While drinking from its elixir
I remember its generosity
To dead leaves
Trying to revive themselves
From its sprightly water
I remember sitting
Under a mapou tree
Envying its freshness
I remember
Its music always clear and joyful
Will I ever hear its song again?
Or have we parted never to meet again?

Walking the same grounds as my ancestors

Who are now guiding me
Lending me a hand
Following in their footsteps
Striving onward is my greatest honor
I feel that I can conquer the world!
Stepping on their shoulders
I can see further and feel reenergized
Knowing that I am now seeing through
The eyes that have already seen it all
Dancing to their old tunes
Listening to their folktales
Realizing through the air we breathe
The whisper of the wind
Communicating as if time-travelling, ending me their ears…
"A beacon of Hope"
The sun and the moon rise and set
The more things change
The more they remain the same
Our ancestors are not really gone
Although invisible to our human eye
They are in our genes
In our surroundings
And forever linked to us…

It was only yesterday

The springtime of my life
I moved into that temple
Spring lasted but one morning!
Soon celebrations for summer tegan:
Dances to the sound of drums
Parades to the sound of trumpets
Long promenades...
intermittent escapades
The summertime of my life:
A festive time indeed!
Soon I grew tired
And fell asleep
In the arms of Morpheus
Then, one afternoon
The cold breeze of Autumn
Awoke me
Not much time
Before winter knocks
At the door of my temple
Will I be ready?

What Should I Say?

What should I say
When, once again, we, two, meet?
I wonder if you would sit
With me by the shore
Help me with my daily chores?
How I long for that day?
What would you do?
Would you hold my hands?
Next to me would you stand?
When life gets tough
Would you hold me tight?
Keep me by your side
Oh! I do, I do, I do!
Forever… forever is my answer!

Fate plays tricks

Finding what one seeks
Longs for so deeply
Can feel
As if being in a maze
Fate does not leave
Anything to chance
Although the path
To one's future
Is paved with unexpected
Twists and turns
One cannot be rattled
Nor live in a haze
One needs to hold its gaze
Cannot pause…
Nor stay arms crossed
Needs to keep moving…
Keep fighting…
Keep searching
Needs unwavering faith
For what will be
Will be
Fate plays tricks
Do not get sick
With flickering doubts

At this stage of the race

All we can think is how to save face
Leave a legacy
Be a little happy
At this point of the game
No longer of concern is fame
Not an option we ponder over
We pray hard to our father who is in heaven
Hallowed be his name
To watch over our loved ones
We treasure little pleasures and are conscious
Of how precious time is: A gift from above!

Some say

Dreams
Do come true
Others say
That
Dreams are true
I dream…
I dream…
I dream of
Stolen moments
The silence of memories
The realm of nothingness
Caught between a rock
And a hard place:
The field of dreams

This is the "Thanks" I get

For leaving my Life behind
To guide your little steps into this World
This is the "Thanks" I get
For giving you a second chance at Life
Come rain...
Come sunshine...
I was there
A woman on a mission
To Guard... Serve...
Protect... Heal...
All my dreams left behind
I Loved wholeheartedly
My wish for Everyone was
Everlasting happiness
This is the "Thanks" I get

Defying all logic

I infused life into that nearly lifeless being
Through the laying of hands…
I begged… I bargained…
Pleaded your case with God
Shared spiritual gifts with you
You became my son
From another mother
Still my flesh and blood
Since that day…
I walked around
With a feeble life force
Our lives became
Cosmically entangled
Today what has
Gotten into you!!!
This is the "Thanks I get"

There was a dark cloud

Looming over the universe
Birds of prey were everywhere
Little did I know that the hands of God were
Holding us and his invisible light
Surrounding us

While you were sleeping

God deployed an army of Angels
To stand at the gate
While we were sleeping
There was a choir of angels
Singing them of beautiful tunes
It was like the tunes were
In synchronization with autumn leaves
Presenting as an offering to God:
The most exquisite choreography
It was mesmerizing
It captured your essence
While you were sleeping
Light overcame darkness
While you were sleeping
That very majestic sign across the sky:
"No weapon formed against you shall prosper"
While you were sleeping
Your most guarded secret was made known to all:
"You are a prized possession of God."
While you were sleeping
Your soul lights up

We were sisters

We were best friends
As long as we had each other
We felt invincible
It was us against the world
We were sisters
Our lives filled with hardships ...
Unfinished symphonies of "I will tell you later
And thank you for thinking of me"
For we had to make ends meet
And time was not on our side
We were sisters
Dreams come undone
Smashed at our feet
At times we were bitter
But our bonds were never broken
As sisters we celebrated...laughed...
And grieved together...
There were moments of bliss and secret sorrows
As passionately we fought... we loved...
Sister, if I had to do it again
Another time...
Another space...Another place...
I would choose you again
And would do better...
Be better!!!
We are sisters
We love deeply
And this forever!!!
We thank God
For Being here for one another
At this particular time...

I hope to see you in my dreams

Navigating through other spiritual realms
Doing random acts of kindness
Spreading happiness…putting a smile
On every celestial being
Earlier when I dozed off
I thought I saw you beaming…
Sitting by a stream
Having a daydream of those loved ones
Left behind…
Miraculously, but, for a moment
I was allowed through the portal
Of your spiritual realm
To collect this message from beyond
To enlighten loved ones: "Love is the answer"
Although dwelling in a higher dimension
You appeared in your human corporeal form
As not to perturb me
You seemed to be at peace
You expressed your gratefulness
For the outpouring of Love
During you sent off
Your message was clear:
"Love is the greatest gift of all"
It can be felt beyond the grave
From one generation to the next
Your life will be Nothing but a blessing
If you let Love be your compass
I will only be one thought away
I can only be reached through Love

Otherwise, I will be lost to you forever…
My passage in your life
will be nothing
But a faded memory
Being blinded by hatred
and greed is not the answer
Being on a different Wavelength
will halt
All communication between us
So, love one another my children

Everybody leaves anyway

Whatever comes my way
I will make headway
Leaving tremendous
Amount of leeway
To explore each day
I will be curious
And take more than a mere stance
Not leaving anything to chance
I will live for today
And make each day worthwhile
While I play there will be plenty of foreplay
I will not ask anyone to stay
For everyone leaves anyway
Someday

God will make a way

Stumbling blocks will vanish
God will have a say
Enemies will be silenced
Trust in the Lord
Do not go astray
All doors shut by the devil will reopen
God Is a God of Miracles
You are very Precious to Him
He knew you before you were born
He knows your heart
God will make a way
He always has the final say!

I will praise you forever...

All the days of my life
What a great sense of relief!
Coming to the realization
That my future is in your hands
What a great sensation!
Completely free to tend
To my occupations
Knowing that you are
Carrying me... guiding me...
Far beyond all human comprehension

It all started with many empty nights

Unfulfilled dreams and broken promises
It all started many winters ago
With long rainy and snowy days
It all started with many foggy nights
Deserted streets and undressed trees
It all started when nature
My most precious companion went on strike
Turning its sun shine into clouds
Clouds... clouds... clouds all over
Hiding a persistent sun struggling
To show its brilliance
Clouds... clouds... clouds... all over
Obscuring a bright star

Thank you, Lord,

For saving me from the grave
I knew that I had be brave
Confront everything with courage
And not be enraged
When they came at me as wild beasts
You kept them from having a feast
Ordering your angels to guard my gate
To save me of the worst fate
A thousand fell at my side
Such a blind side!
You kept your word
My Lord, the conqueror
You forgave and erased all my errors
God, my promise keeper

I call upon the grace of God to cover me

His favor to find me
I call upon love to be my compass
The Light of God to shine on me forever
I call upon prosperity to be my faithful companion
And scarcity never to cross my path
I call upon Jehovah Jireh
My Lord the provider
I call upon Jehovah Nissi
My mighty Warrior
Scatter of enemies, Lord of Victory
My God who never fails
I call upon Jehovah Rapha
My God, the Healer
To restore my body and soul
Lead me beside the still waters
I call upon Jehovah Rohi
My God, my Shepherd
The provider and protector
In whom I trust completely
For I shall not want
I call upon my magnificent father
To surround me with a bright light
To blind the eyes of my enemies
So, no weapon forged
Against me shall succeed

I call upon my energy

From all the corners of the Universe
Wherever it is left to return
I call upon all pieces of myself scattered
Through the laying of hands...
Supplications...Incantations...
Out of body experiences...Sexual encounters...
To return
I cut all invisible cords
That no longer serve my journey
I command my spirit
To no longer waste energy
On the ungrateful
And the wicked
I ask God to renew my spirit
Restore my energy
Lessen my burden
So, I can step into the shoes of my destiny
Complete my mission here on earth...
Your work is plentiful...
There are few workers, Father!

I will not let go!

I will hold on to you
Dear Life, My Life...
I am all in
Me, myself and I
I will be blessed
Till the day I die
I will honor and cherish you
My Life...My existence...
My time here on earth...
Even if I fall
I will have the final world
Rule my world!
After all, this is my story
Master of my destiny
I will never ever relinquish power
Step aside! Out of sight!!! Captain of my own ship
I, only can decide who boards my boat...
Sails across the sea of my life
Only I can sink or stay afloat
I am not afraid of storms
For, I have learned to sail with the tide
At times... even, against current...
I dance to the rhythm of the waves
I am quite skilled at surviving
This is my story, only I can write the ending:
I choose to be happy!

Longtemps je t'ai attendu

J'ai parcouru un si long chemin
Qu'est-ce qui t'as retardé?
Juste pour un instant
J'ai cru que tu n'allais plus arriver
Tout ce parcours tumultueux sans toi
J'ai traversé tant d'océans…
Visité d'autres horizons…
Dans le silence des nuits
Mon coeur endolori a saigné de douleur
Témoin de ton parchemin sacré:
Mon corps se faisant effleurer
Qu'est-ce qui t'as tant retenu?
A peine jour dans ton monde
Qu'il commence déjà à faire nuit dans le mien
Dans ton monde
C'est si bruyant!
Il fait chaud…très chaud…
D'une chaleur de diable
A en couper le souffle…
Pourtant dans mon monde,
Tout est calme!
Au crépuscule de ma vie
Avec des yeux qui ont déjà tout vu
Rien n'ébranle!
Âme soeur!
Flamme jumelle!
Est-ce la fin de nos voyages
A travers le temps?

D'un clignement d'oeil rapide

Nos regards se croisent
Un petit bonjour
Pour un petit flirt avec moi
La magie du début!
Le début d'une orageuse aventure
Remplie de douces fessées...
De mots sensuels...
Tous mes sens en eveil !!!
Enfin c'était mon tour...
Une chance pour "notre pour toujours"
Il ne m'avait meme pas fait la cour
Pourtant un avenir aspirant
Suivi d'un depart inopiné
Un si long détour
Un désir pressant de renouer
D'amour de feu et de passion
Un retour sans fin
Quelle joie immense!

Can you wash away the scent of the other woman?

What does she have that I don't?
Is it the wiggle of the hips?
Why is her fragrance all over you?
The taste of her nectar breaking news?
Is the walk of shame your portion for me?
Aren't I worthy in your eyes?
They talk behind my back
And see me as "le dindon de la farce"
Is it the weight of time written all over my face?
My soothing and calm voice
Or my slow and calm demeanor?
Is that what gave them licenses to degrade me?
How long will you let them insult me?
They returned ungratefulness for kindness
Mistook gentleness for weakness
They came to bury me but I rose as a phoenix
Forewarned is forearmed!

Epouse effacée

Femme blessée jusqu'aux os
A qui on donne des coups
Mais qui reste jusqu'au bout
Reprends goût à la vie!
Entre dans les parvis de Dieu
Avec des louanges. Ouvres les yeux!
Tu mérites mieux!
Épouse en arrière plan
A qui on ne donne pas son temps
Mais qui mérite d'être cajolée
Femme dont la présence dérange
Épouse qu'on arrache le cœur
Mais qui force le bonheur
Celle qui donne plus qu'elle ne reçoit
Sans estime de soi!
Aies confiance en toi
Femme en cœur de miettes
Qui croit n'avoir rien dans son assiette
Femme a la dérive, seule au milieu d'une tempête
Mène to bateau à bon port
N'accepte pas ce sort!
Épouse dépassée qui cache ses blessures
Sans aucune protection des éclaboussures
Épouse pillée qui essaie de recommencer
Apprends à t'aimer
Tiens les rênes de ta vie
Tu mérites d'être vue
Laisse ta lumière briller

www.ingramcontent.com/pod-product-compliance
Lightning Source LLC
Chambersburg PA
CBHW050330010526
44119CB00050B/736